A Note to Parents

DK READERS is a compelling program for beginning readers, designed in conjunction with leading literacy experts, including Dr. Linda Gambrell, Director of the Eugene T. Moore School of Education at Clemson University. Dr. Gambrell has served on the Board of Directors of the International Reading Association and as President of the National Reading Conference.

Beautiful illustrations and superb full-color photographs combine with engaging, easy-to-read stories to offer a fresh approach to each subject in the series. Each DK READER is guaranteed to capture a child's interest while developing his or her reading skills, general knowledge, and love of reading.

The five levels of DK READERS are aimed at different reading abilities, enabling you to choose the books that are exactly right for your child:

Pre-level 1: Learning to read
Level 1: Beginning to read
Level 2: Beginning to read alone
Level 3: Reading alone
Level 4: Proficient readers

The "normal" age at which a child begins to read can be anywhere from three to eight years old, so these levels are only a general guideline.

No matter which level you select, you can be sure that you are helping your child learn to read, then read to learn!

LONDON, NEW YORK, MUNICH,
MELBOURNE, AND DELHI

Series Editor Deborah Lock
Managing Art Editor Clare Shedden
U.S. Editor Elizabeth Hester
Senior DTP Designer Almudena Díaz
Production Allison Lenane
Picture Researcher Marie Ortu
Jacket Designer Katy Wall

Reading Consultant
Linda Gambrell, Ph.D.

First American Edition, 2005
14 15 14 13 12 11
Published in the United States by DK Publishing
345 Hudson Street, New York, New York 10014
016-DD251-Aug/2005

Published in Great Britain by Dorling Kindersley Limited

Library of Congress Cataloging-in-Publication Data
Durant, Penny Raife.
Sniffles, sneezes, hiccups, and coughs / written by Penny Durant.--
1st American ed.
    p. cm. -- (Dk readers. Level 2)
Includes bibliographical references and index.
ISBN-13: 978-0-7566-1107-1   ISBN-10: 0-7566-1107-5 (PLC)
ISBN-13: 978-0-7566-1106-4   ISBN-10: 0-7566-1106-7 (PB)
1. Respiration--Juvenile literature. 2. Sneezing--Juvenile literature.
3. Cough--Juvenile literature. 4. Hiccups--Juvenile literature. I.
Title. II. Dorling Kindersley readers. 2, Beginning to read alone
QP121.D8655 2005
612.2--dc22

                                    2005001105

Color reproduction by Colourscan, Singapore
Printed and bound in China by L. Rex Printing Co., Ltd.

The publisher would like to thank the following for
their kind permission to reprduce their images:
Position key: =above; b=bottom, c=center; l=left; r=right; t=top.
2 Alamy Images: Stock Connection Distribution (br); **Getty Images:** Dennis
O'Clair (tr); **Science Photo Library:** Lea Paterson (cr). **3 Science Photo Library:**
Damien Lovegrove (tr). **4 Ardea.com:** John Daniels (cl). **6 Corbis:** Kevin Fleming.
9 Alamy Images: Natural Visions (main); **Science Photo Library:** David Scharf
(tr). **10-11 Photolibrary.com:** Leanne Temme. **11 Science Photo Library:**
Damien Lovegrove (t). **12 Science Photo Library:** Gusto Productions.
13 Science Photo Library: Gusto Productions. **14-15 Science Photo Library:**
Dr. John Brackenbury (background). **15 Alamy Images:** Guy Spangenberg (tr).
16 Science Photo Library: Dr. Gopal Murti (tr). **16-17 Corbis:** LWA-Stephen
Welstead (b). **20 Science Photo Library:** Mark Clarke. **22 Alamy Images:**
Jan Stromme (tr). **26 Warren Photographic. 27 Corbis:** Wally McNamee (tl);
Science Photo Library: Lea Paterson (b). **28 Corbis:** Galen Rowell (br).
28-29 Getty Images: Jim Cummins. **31 Alamy Images:** Ace Stock Limited.
32 Bubbles: Ian West (tr).

All other images © Dorling Kindersley Limited
For futher information see: www.dkimages.com

Discover more at
www.dk.com

DK READERS

BEGINNING
TO READ ALONE
2

Sniffles, Sneezes, Hiccups, and Coughs

Written by Penny Durant

DK Publishing

Ah -

Ah-choo!
Everyone sneezes—people,
dogs, cats, horses, turtles,
birds, and even giraffes!
Some sneezes are loud.
Others are quiet.

Some people sneeze again
and again.
But why do we all sneeze?

And why do we cough,
hiccup, and yawn, too?

choo!

You breathe to take in the air
your body needs.

Your nose and mouth are both
passageways for air to get into
your body.

The air travels past your throat
and into the airways
that lead to your lungs.

Your diaphragm, chest muscles,
and brain work together to keep air
going in and out of your lungs.

Diaphragm
This muscle is springy
like a trampoline.
It pulls down and
pushes up as you
breathe in and out.

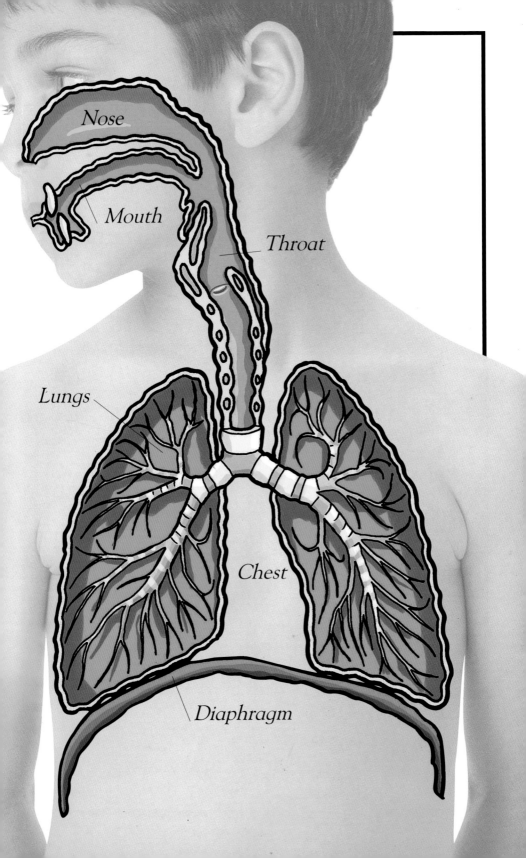

Nose

Mouth

Throat

Lungs

Chest

Diaphragm

The airways to your lungs need
to be kept clear all the time.
When you breathe in through
your nose, your tiny nose hairs
filter the air, and the sticky mucus
(snot) collects anything that could
be harmful.
It might be dust or pepper or pollen.

House dust

A speck of dust is not just dirt but a mixture of different things, such as skin flakes, hair, food crumbs, and dust mites.

You feel a tickle.
Your body does not
want these things
in your nose.
Your brain tells
your body to sneeze.

You sneeze more often when
you have a cold.
Germs collect in your nose
and make it tickle and swell.

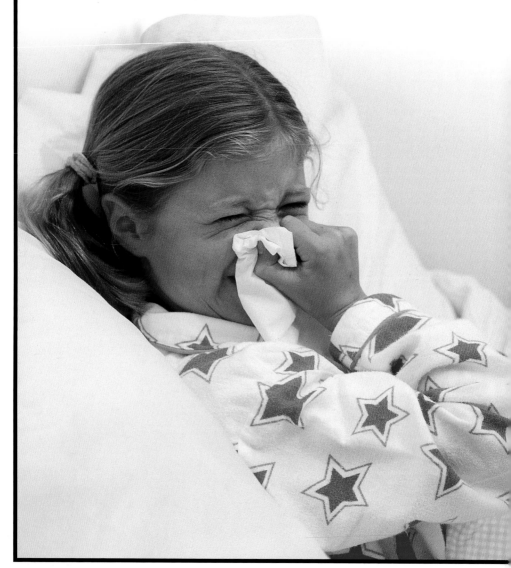

Sneezing gets rid of the germs,
but they can be spread to
other people this way.

Sneezing into a tissue
stops the germs
from spreading.
Some people sneeze
when they go out
into sunlight.
No one knows why.

Ahhhh...

When you sneeze, you take
a deep breath.
(That is the "ah" part.)
You hold your breath as
your chest muscles tighten.
The pressure of the air in
your lungs increases.
You close your eyes.

...choo!

Your tongue presses against
the roof of your mouth.
Suddenly your breath comes out
fast through your nose.
(That is the "choo" part.)

Your sneeze could be traveling
at a speed of 100 miles (161 km)
per hour!

The gush of air blows
the dust or germs—
and the tickle—out
of your nose.

Let it out!
A sneeze travels as fast as a speeding car, so never try to stop it by holding your nose. The pressure can injure your ears.

Water droplets, mucus, dust, and germs are forced out of your nose.

But what happens if the pollen, dust, or germs get caught in your throat or in the airways to your lungs? Then a message is sent to your brain to tell your body to cough.

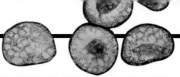

Invaders

Germs are tiny living things that can cause diseases. If they get into your body, they can make you sick.

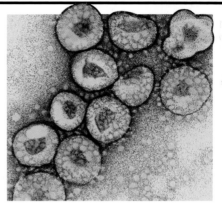

When you have a cold, you may feel stuffed up with phlegm [FLEM]. Phlegm is thick, sticky mucus. It picks up the germs that have reached your lungs and airways. The phlegm needs to be cleared out so you can breathe better. This is why you cough.

Remember to cover your mouth with your hand when you cough to stop the germs from spreading to someone else.

Your vocal cords are open for breathing.

When you cough, you take a deep breath and hold it, while your chest and stomach muscles tighten.

Then your diaphragm pushes
the air out of your lungs.
The sudden gush of air carries
the pollen, dust, or phlegm
out of your mouth.
As the air rushes over your open
vocal cords, they vibrate and
make a sound.
Your cough might
sound like a dog
barking.

Hic. Hic. Hic.

You've got the hiccups.

This may happen if you drink drinks
with bubbles or you eat too quickly.

Your diaphragm tightens
in a jerky way.

It pulls in sharply and you take
a quick gulp of air.

Your vocal cords are closed.

They are not ready for the breath.

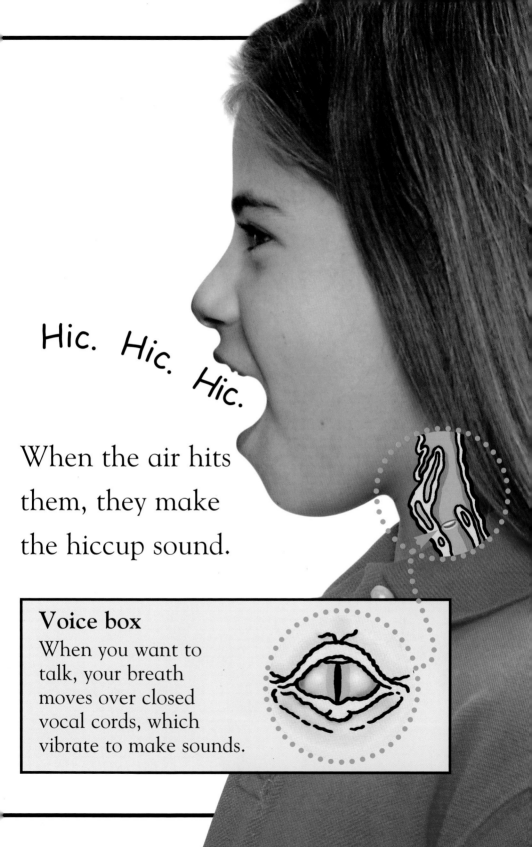

Hic. Hic. Hic.

When the air hits
them, they make
the hiccup sound.

Voice box
When you want to
talk, your breath
moves over closed
vocal cords, which
vibrate to make sounds.

You hiccupped
even before you
were born.
No one knows
why we hiccup,
but people try
lots of different

things to get rid of them.
Some people hold their breath.
Some breathe in and
out of a paper bag.

*A paper bag
can help you
control your
breathing.*

Some people drink water.

Some put sugar on their tongues.

Some people think if you are scared
or startled, you will stop hiccuping.

*Some people bend
over and drink
water upside down.*

If I yawn, will you yawn?
Probably.
Just thinking about yawning
can make you yawn.
When you yawn,
you open your mouth
very wide.

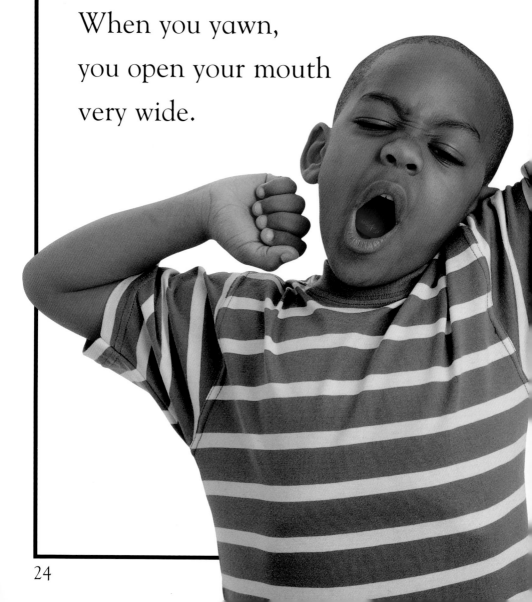

Your jaw opens
and stretches your face
and neck muscles.
You might close your eyes.
You take in a deep breath
to fill your lungs.
Then you let it out.

Huge yawns
Hippopotamuses
can open their
jaws up to
an angle of
150 degrees.

Why do you yawn?
You yawn when you are sleepy,
but also when you wake up.

Warm-up exercise
Athletes yawn before a race.
Musicians yawn before a
concert. Yawning and
stretching make us alert and
ready for something new.

You might yawn if you are bored,
but also when you are not.
Maybe it is your body's way of saying,
"Let's do something different."

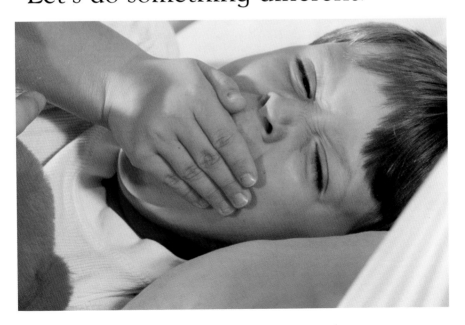

Oxygen is in the air that
you breathe.
Your whole body needs oxygen
to change the food you eat
into energy.
In your lungs, oxygen enters
your bloodstream and then
travels around your body
to where it is needed.
Usually you breathe
without even noticing.

Breathing out
The air you breathe out
has carbon dioxide that
your body does not need.
Plants use carbon dioxide
to make their food.

You breathe more deeply when you are exercising, because you need more oxygen.

Sometimes you may want to control your breath.

You can blow bubbles, pant to cool down, or breathe very slowly.

Maybe you can whistle by forcing your breath through the small opening of your lips.

Your body is a marvelous machine.

Remember this the next time
you yawn
or get the hiccups
or cough
or sneeze.
Ah, ah, ah . . . *choo!*

Breathing facts

We lose one pint (half a liter) of
water every day through breathing.
We see this water vapor when
we breathe onto glass or outside
in cold air.

Insects breathe air through a few
openings in their abdomen (belly)
called spiracles. They have no lungs.

Adult bullfrogs breathe in
80 percent of the air they
need through their thin skin.

Some people think that
sneezing is a sign of good luck.
Others think of it as
a warning of death.

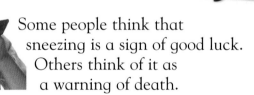

Donna Griffiths from Worcestershire, England, had
the longest recorded sneezing fit. It lasted 978 days.
At the beginning, she sneezed once every minute.

Charles Osborne from Iowa holds the record for the
longest hiccup attack. He hiccupped over 20 times
a minute for 68 years—from 1922 until 1990.